A BRIEF HISTORY OF WEYMOUTH St. PAUL'S HARRIERS & AC

1889 - 1991

David Bucke

Copyright © 2017 David Bucke

All rights reserved.

ISBN-10: 1544211686
ISBN-13: 978-1544211688

CONTENTS

CONTENTS iii

ACKNOWLEDGMENTS v

1. INTRODUCTION 1

2. EARLY DAYS 3

3. THE NINETEEN-THIRTIES 17

4. THE NINETEEN-FORTIES 21

5. THE POST WORLD WAR II PERIOD 23

6. CUP AND TROPHIES 31

7. THE NINETEEN SEVENTIES 35

8. THE NINETEEN EIGHTIES 49

9. THE NINETEEN NINETIES 77

THE AUTHOR 87

INDEX 89

ACKNOWLEDGMENTS

Information in the text:

John Powell, Brian Dunn, Joe Townsend, Pete Hammond, T.J. Copp, Mrs. Airey, Harry Dowell, Val Palmer, Geoff Kirby, Tom Hutchins, Mrs. Doreen Higgs, Brian James of Bournemouth AC, Bill Fellowes, Harry Callow, Mike Baggs, Evelyn Morris, John Bolton, Beryl Keele.

Figures:

Mrs. Airey, Mrs D Higgs, B. Dunn, H. Dowell, G. Hunwicks, D. Bucke and F.J. Blackford.

The picture of Percy Hodge on page 11 is in the public domain - http://bit.ly/2m6ZhfH

The providers of a few pictures could not be identified, contacted or are deceased.

Map:

The map on page 4 is © OpenStreetMap contributors - see http://www.openstreetmap.org/copyright

The author apologizes for omissions in the above information.

1. INTRODUCTION

This Athletics or "Pedestrianism", as it was then known, was becoming a popular sport in the 19th Century. Harrier clubs were springing up in many of the towns and cities.

Possibly the sportsmen (there were no lady athletes then) were spurred on by the exploits of famous runners of the day such as W.G. George, the world mile record holder in 1896, with a time of 4 min 12.7 sec.

Or perhaps it was the revival of the Olympic Games that same year, 1896.

Whatever the reason, what of the Harrier clubs that were established in Victorian times?

How many have survived today?

Who were the members of the clubs?

What sort of performances did they do? Those and many other questions are posed when someone takes on the task of writing up the history of a club.

I arrived in Weymouth in 1977 and joined the only club then in existence in the town, Weymouth St. Paul's Harriers and Athletic Club. I had recently left my old club, the Cambridge and Coleridge Athletics Club, which had its interesting history written up, and it did not take me long to realise that the Weymouth St. Paul's Harriers (WSPH) history went back into the last Century.

If I met a Weymouthian invariably the conversation would get round to athletics. It was surprising how many of them said their parents, grandparents, or other relatives were once members of

INTRODUCTION

the Harriers. My former running companion with the Harriers was Brian Dunn. He told me so much about the exploits of the Harriers of yesteryear - and Brian would know, as he was until recently, an active runner for over 50 years with the club!

All of this made me interested to find out more about the Club's history. However, such research takes time, something we all seem short of these days. I proposed to the Club's Committee that a history of the Club should be written and with some research from an ex-member, Pete Hammond in 1989, a first draft was prepared by the then Hon. Sec., Val Palmer.

The first draft was handed back to me to finish. I started, but ran out of time, and the history was put aside. After several more attempts, I have written what I hope is still interesting, although incomplete. Of course, the 'centenary' has now passed.

Pete Hammond wrote a considerable number of letters to old members, and looked up many references in Weymouth Town Library. The outcome was that loaned photographs and newspaper cuttings arrived.

At least I had a base to start from and acknowledgements to as many people as I can remember are made on page v. If you are not mentioned please forgive me, your help was appreciated.

Weymouth Public Library was the first port of call for this research, and it became obvious that information about 19th century Harriers in Weymouth was sparse.

The Weymouth Red Book (1905), which was the official Borough Annual, listed the inauguration of Weymouth's clubs and societies, as well as the dates of important social and historical events in the town. Weymouth Harriers is listed as being formed in 1889, although there is an earlier date of 1869 - which I believe to be a misprint.

The late Joe Townsend was a fount of knowledge on historical and sports events in the town and he passed on some interesting facts about the Club, including some about Weymouth's first Olympic Gold medallist, Percy Hodge.

Aside from talking to ex-members, the archives of local newspapers provided considerable information and I found out a lot more from looking at the inscriptions on the many cups and trophies belonging to the Club.

2. EARLY DAYS

One of my Hardy's Hash House Harrier friends pointed out an early reference to Harriers in Weymouth in a 'History of Weymouth College to 1901' by C.G. Faulkner.

There is a single paragraph on page 76 referring to the year 1884:

> *"An account of one of the usual paper-chases, in which the 'hares' ran down the Preston Road - up over the "plough" behind the coastguards' station - forded the Jordan river - on through Preston and Sutton Poyntz - up over Reservoir Hill - skirting Came Wood with its brambles - over plough and grassland to Winterbourne Monkton - entered a covered waterway - on over more grassland - up over the Ridgeway a mile to the west of the tunnel - down through Upwey, and back home along the turnpike road".*

A distance of about 14 miles - see the map on the following page!

The official "Weymouth Red Book, 1905", a gazette of local history and events, lists Weymouth Harriers to have been formed in 1889. No historical details between 1889 and 1905 are given, although, there is the dubious 1869 date, which I think is a mistake.

In 1905, the Club Captain was Mr. G. Condliffe; Hon. Sec., Mr L.C. Damon, 49, St. Thomas Street, Weymouth.

Club runs were on Wednesday evenings. There were no fixed headquarters.

In conjunction with Weymouth Bicycle Club, a race meeting was held every August.

It's not much to go on, but at least this positive entry gave me a

EARLY DAYS

starting point.

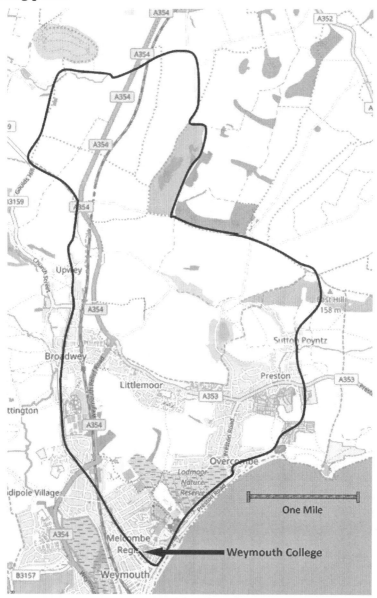

A typical fourteen mile paper chase by boys of Weymouth College in the 1880s.

Furthermore, the connection with the Bicycle Club was interesting, because there was obviously a sporting link. Bicycles were expensive, although popular in Edwardian days, yet there

EARLY DAYS

must have been many fit young men who could not afford them, and foot running was the obvious alternative as it was free!

Weymouth Bicycle Club was formed in 1875, and amongst its many officers was Mr. H.A. Hurdle, a well known butcher in Weymouth as well as a musician, being the organist in St Mary's church for many years. The H.A. Hurdle cup was presented to Westham St Paul's Harriers in 1904, to be awarded to the winner of the Club's annual 10 mile race. The cup is still in existence, but has been renamed the T.G. Copp cup. More of that later!

I was contacted by John Powell, a sports historian (who used to be a member of St Paul's Harriers in the early 1980s, competing in race walking events). He informed me that the date 1889 was most likely correct for Weymouth Harriers. He stated that Westham St Paul's Harriers were formed in 1906, which I think is incorrect, because we have an engraved cup for 1904, as mentioned above. Weymouth YMCA Harriers were formed in 1906 and Dorchester YMCA Harriers, in 1903.

It is on record that Dorset Police Sports were held from 1896 and they became open events in 1907. In the years 1904 and 1905, Poole Shop Assistants held sports in Poole Park (around the cycle track) and both Weymouth Harriers and Dorchester YMCA Harriers competed.

In 1912, there was a road race challenge for the Hambro Cup. The four clubs competing were Dorchester YMCA Harriers, Weymouth YMCA Harriers, Westham St. Paul's Harriers and Weymouth Town Harriers! In 1914, the Hambro Challenge cup race took part again, but without Weymouth Town Harriers - I have no further information on Weymouth Town Harriers.

St. Paul's Harriers was part of the St. Paul's church boys' club in Abbotsbury Road, Weymouth. St. Paul's church was built around 1900. Activities of the boys' sports club included football, gymnastics, boxing and athletics. According to John Powell's research, Westham St. Paul's Harriers became known as Weymouth St. Paul's Harriers in 1929. Presumably, Weymouth Harriers ceased sometime before then.

This information seemed to be backed up because in the South Dorset Labour Sports, T. Costello competed in the 440 yds. in $56\,^2/_5$ secs in 1920 and F.J. Miller ran the same event in 1921. Both athletes ran for Westham St Paul's Harriers.

EARLY DAYS

Canon Martin Fisher was the inspiration behind the church boys' club and he featured in the early photographs of both Westham and Weymouth St. Paul's Harriers for a number of years. He was an Oxford Blue which was awarded for rowing. He joined the church in 1906. According to a church leaflet listing events over its century, St. Paul's Harriers was formed in 1906. However, the Hurdle Cup has its presentation date to the Harriers as 1904.

1907 - 1920s

"Hambro" Challenge Cup races between Weymouth YMCA, Westham St. Paul's Harriers and Dorchester YMCA Harriers. The start of the race was at the King's Statue were held in the early 1900s.

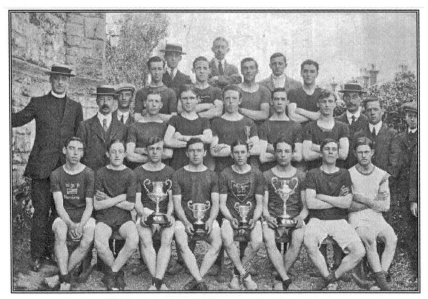

Figure 1: 1909 - St. Paul's Harriers

The Rev. Martin Fisher is standing on the left.

Note the Hurdle cup held by the Harrier 3rd front left.

In this 1909 picture of St Paul's Harriers, note that the athletes did not have the familiar present day white vest with its green horizontal band. It was a dark, black short-sleeved vest with a triangular badge incorporating a five barred gate with "W St P Harriers" embroidered on the front.

This early photograph shows the Club with its founder and

EARLY DAYS

obvious link with St Paul's Church, Canon Martin Fisher on the left, and several well known runners of the day. Notably, is George Thomas Bugler 3rd from the left in the front row.

It is worth examining the details of this excellent photograph. The four cups include the Hurdle Challenge 10 mile Cup, on the left. No doubt the winners, whose names are engraved on the shields on the bases of the cups, are in the picture. All the runners and attendants are neatly attired, fit and alert looking. Canon Martin Fisher was the 1st WSPH club President.

One WSP Harrier who might have been in that photograph was Tom Hutchins. Tom wrote a letter to Pete Hammond in 1989 when he was 96 years old, and living in Milton Keynes.

Tom Hutchins wrote again, this time to me in June, 1991, informing me that he was not in any of the pre-1912 photographs I sent him for his school lectures, because he was already in the army by then!

Figure 2: Circa 1910 - St. Paul's Church Boys Club Gymnastic display by members.

Tom was a former member of St. Paul's Harriers and competed regularly. He was born and lived in Emmerdale Road, Weymouth and remembered the course that the Harriers used to run. He said that the races used to start at St Paul's Church, Westham, and out to Chickerell and back. He also mentioned his runs in the "marathon" (really a 10 miles race) to Portland and back for a silver Cup. The "Hurdle" Cup no less! However, Tom said he did not ever win the Cup, because he said he was not a very good runner.

Tom's letter contains reminiscences of his youth in Weymouth, including being a goalkeeper for Westham Football Club. His brother was also a Harrier.

George Bugler, a former club captain, is seen clearer in the photograph dated 1914 (below). (The great, grand-father of Mark Puckett, a Harrier in the 1980's). This picture was taken to celebrate the winning of the Hambro Cup.

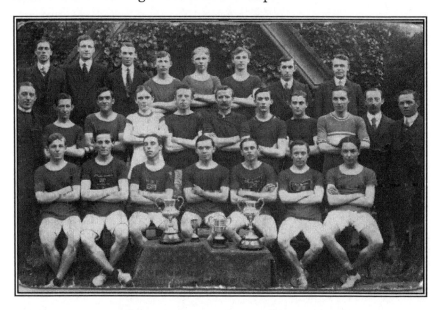

Figure 3: 1914 - St. Paul's Harriers

Back row: F. Payne, L. Uncles, H. Young, R. Hall, C. Bartlett, T. Keech, R. Bagell, T. Bagell,

Middle row: Rev. M. Fisher, F. Palmer, B. Woodwood, T. Welland, S. Bridgeman, W. Barret, N. Reed, H. Shaw, E. Lovell, W. Symonds (Handicap Sec.), T. Prinhead (Hon. Sec and Treasurer)

Front row: W. Anderson, R. Brown, R.T Wellman, G. Bugler (Capt.), C. Nes (Sub Capt.) W. Brantingham, R. Lovell.

As stated above, St. Paul's Harriers was formed around the beginning of the 20th century, but whether it was a separate club from the earlier formed Weymouth Harriers is confusing.

EARLY DAYS

Newspaper reports of the day often only refer to "Harriers".

I have a little history about Weymouth YMCA Harriers from a photocopy of that Club's fixture card for 1911, which makes some interesting reading.

WEYMOUTH
Y.M.C.A HARRIERS

OFFICERS

President:

Rev. T. Lancaster, M.A.

Vice-Presidents

E. P. Rogers, Esq   P. D. A. Courtnay, Esq.

Chairman of Committee:

F. E. Abbot. Esq

Captain:

Mr. J. B. Griffiths

Sub-Captain:

Mr. E. G. R. Bartlett

Hon. Sec. & Treas: Hon. Asst. Sec:

Mr. R. G. Bray   Mr. W. E. Bray

Committee:

Messrs. B. Biles, F. Barnicoat, G. Buglar

G. A. Hawkes, and H. S. Wotherspoon

H. D. Warwick, Printer, Weymouth

Figure 4: Cover of the YMCA Harriers Rule Book from 1911.

Whether both clubs amalgamated is not clear, but I know that some runners were members of both clubs. Weymouth YMCA

EARLY DAYS

Harriers competed regularly against Dorchester YMCA Harriers for the Hambro Cup. Figure 4 shows the Committee members of the time.

Figure 5: 1911 - Weymouth YMCA Harriers

Sub-Captain E.G.R. Bartlett is sitting 2nd right second row. Reverend T. Lancaster, President is middle left.

There were 14 General Rules, including the Club Colours — Royal Blue and Black.

Subscriptions were 1 Shilling (5p) per annum.

The club's headquarters were in Frederick Place - with practice, cross-country races and on the roads from 1st October - until 30th. April.

Also, on club runs, a "Pacemaker" was appointed by the Captain, and no-one was allowed to pass the pacemaker without the consent of the Captain.

The fixture list informs us that the runs started at 8.30 pm prompt each Wednesday, and some Saturdays. The distances were from 1.5 miles to the then classic 10 miles. Examples of the courses included:

1) St Thomas St., St. Edmond St., Mitchell St., seafront and around Westerall - 1.5 miles.

EARLY DAYS

2) The Village Blacksmith, Broadwey, and return - 4 miles.

3) Chalbury Lodge, and return - 5 miles.

and so on.......

Another interesting fact is that the fixture card was printed by H.D. Warwick, Weymouth.

Over the years the Harriers have used that firm a few times for their fixture cards!

Figure 6: 1920 - Percy Hodge winning Gold in the 3,000 m Olympic Steeplechase [1].

In 1912, a very fine runner took up residence in Weymouth. His name was Percy Hodge. Hodge was born in Guernsey.

According to the Guernsey Evening Post, July 10, 1912, Bournemouth AC held their annual sports, which included the one mile flat race championships.

This race incorporated the new AAAs districts, Hampshire, Wiltshire, Dorset, the Isle of Wight and the Channel Islands.

The race was won by J.F. Wadmore (Ravensbourne, London) and Percy Hodge was second, with R. Edwards (Reading AC) 3rd.

The winner's time was 4 min. 39.2 secs.

Percy ran in Weymouth YMCA Harriers' colours in that race.

The newspaper article states that Percy was already the Dorset half-mile and one mile champion, but in this Bournemouth race he did not do himself justice.

Well justice did eventually come to Percy when he went on to compete in the 1920 Olympic Games in Antwerp Belgium, won a

---

1. https://en.wikipedia.org/wiki/Percy_Hodge

Gold in the 3000 metres steeplechase.

His 1st place was outstanding in many ways because he had to run in a heat which he won in 10 mins 17.4 secs which was a new Olympic record. In the final he bettered his Olympic record with a time of 10 mins 00.4 secs.

He won the race by 100 yards from Pat Hyne (USA), with Ernesto Ambrosini (Italy) 3rd.

Percy Hodge competed regularly in Weymouth Police Sports, which were held at the town's football ground, Marsh Road. He also competed in the Dorset Constabulary Sports, held at Dorchester.

He was an AAA champion in 2 miles steeplechase from 1919 to 1921 and in 1923.

In 1920 his shoe fell off in the second lap causing him to stop and lose some 100 yards, yet he won the race by a margin of 75 yards.

He also finished ninth at the International Cross Country Championships and helped his team to win a first place earlier in 1920.

The only other UK winner of the Olympic steeplechase was Chris Brasher.

Percy Hodge is buried in his native Guernsey.

The Ups And Downs Of "Weymouth Harriers"

An interesting article appeared in the "Southern Times" (5th April, 1924) about a meeting on the demise of the Weymouth Harriers Club.

Apparently the Hon Sec. of the newly formed Dorset Amateur Athletic Association, Mr. R. C. Cox, had called a special meeting at the Guildhall to try and arouse interest in re-establishing the Harriers in the town, because interest had been "dead".

There was some discussion about whether the Club should affiliate to the County organization but it was pointed out that there were no Harriers present at the meeting, although they had been invited.

Therefore, it was proposed to call another meeting to reform the Harriers Club.

This is interesting because Frank Miller, a well known Weymouth

EARLY DAYS

athlete, left Westham St. Paul's Harriers in 1924 and joined Poole Harriers.

Then in 1927, he re-joined Westham St. Paul's Harriers! It could have been because his work as a policeman took him away from Weymouth.

Figures 7 and 8 below show that the Harriers were not defunct.

Figure 7: Circa 1927 – Harriers

Front row: Christie, T.G Copp, unknown, F. Miller

Second row: unknown, Mr Symonds, Rev. M. Fisher, unknown, unknown, unknown

Third row: not identified, except for F. Damen, 3rd from right.

Back row: all unidentified.

The Club team photograph, above, shows members in the club colours of today.

Canon Martin Fisher and other officials seen in earlier photos are proudly standing or sitting with the athletes.

Important and popular sports events were held in the town in the late 1920s. These events were usually promoted by the local Constabulary. It is worth noting that at one of those meetings, Supt. F. Miller, Insp.E. Lovell as well as Mr. H.H Wheldon, Secretary of Weymouth F.C. were present.

EARLY DAYS

Frank Miller won the Hambro Challenge Cup race in 1929, still running for Westham St. Paul's Harriers. This was the year that Westham St. Paul's Harriers became Weymouth St. Paul's Harriers.

Figure 8: About 1929 – WSP Harriers

Back Row: Unknown, Darch, F. Damen, unknown

Front Row: Unknown, Unknown, F. Miller (holding the Loyalty Cup), T.G. Copp (holding the other cup), unknown

Figure 9: Start of the Southampton - Bournemouth Road Relay 1929. Bill Fellowes is arrowed.

The sports meetings in Weymouth were held in those days at the

EARLY DAYS

old Weymouth Town FC ground. There must have been rapid response from the Harriers because there are many newspaper reports of team and individual athletic achievements in the 1920's.

Bill Fellowes was a Club member in the 1920's and sent some interesting newspaper cuttings and photographs to prove that the Harriers were not "dead".

Figure 10: 1926 - Two WSPH past Presidents
Front with Ball: Fred Babb
Back Right: Colonel C.F. Linnett

EARLY DAYS

3. THE NINETEEN-THIRTIES

The name T.G. Copp crops up many times in athletic reports during the 1930's. Mr Copp was a staunch member, and competitive runner for the Harriers. Just before he died in 1988, he wrote a very interesting letter to me especially for this history.

T.G. Copp started his athletics career with Dorchester YMCA Harriers. He was their club captain for many years, winning their Ashley Cup in 1926.

Dorchester YMCA Harriers closed down in 1927 for a few years, and it was during this break that T.G. Copp switched his allegiance to St Paul's Harriers, where he was a long-time proud member.

However, he was something of a controversial person because, on the reformation of Dorchester YMCA Harriers, he re-joined that club. He was again elected Club Captain, but as he would not resign from Weymouth St Paul's Harriers, where he was now a first claim member, the Dorset AAAs suspended him for six months.

In the end Copp opted to compete for St Paul's Harriers.

T.G. Copp was a leading runner for the Harriers in both road and cross-country races. He won the Hurdle Challenge Cup in 1929, 1930, and 1932. This hat trick of wins, which in the Club rules of those days, allowed him to retain the Cup as his own property. T.G. Copp helped the Harriers win the Hambro Cup, which was one of the most sought after trophies in South Dorset, in 1929, 1931 and 1933.

He was first on two occasions and second three times. He won the Weatheral Cup two years running, almost competing the hat-trick

THE NINETEEN-THIRTIES

again, but was beaten by 10 yards by team mate Handal. (Handal, I believe came from Dorchester).

It appears that Copp's role in team running was to do the pace-making, which he did in this latter race, leading all the way until he reached the sea-front, when Handal swept by him right at the end before the Pavilion.

T.G. Copp informed me that Weymouth St Paul's Harriers was very strong in the 1930's, with Darch, Tucker and Miller all being track champions. The Club was active in road-running and cross-country in the winter.

The cross-country races were held over Lodmoor, and many of the road races were held on Portland (there was no separate club there then!). Track races were held against Bournemouth AC, Poole Wheelers and the Royal Navy AC. The track was on Weymouth Football ground. The Club President was still Canon Martin Fisher. Club Secretary was Mr. Dunford who joined the church as a clergyman.

The Treasurer was Mr. Brookes and the Handicapper was Mr. Symonds. T.G. Copp represented Weymouth St Paul's Harriers on the Dorset AAA's Committee, and organised three Dorset County Track and Field Championships at Dorchester, as well as track races at Dorchester Football Club ground. County races in those days had entries around 350 (Bournemouth AC was not then in the County).

Copp was also a qualified track judge and officiated at many meetings in the area. For example, he helped organise the Dorset Agricultural Sports, and the TUC World Sports and Games at Dorchester Recreation Ground.

In 1937, he was asked to form Dorchester AC, which included the Girls' Green School, Hardye's School and other local youngsters. Therefore, through Weymouth St Paul's Harriers, there were links with Dorchester YMCA, and Dorchester AC.

T.G. Copp lists a number of his St Paul's team mates: Fred Damen, Hibbs, Handal, Frank Miller, William Miller, R. Russell, K. Spring, Parry-Gill, Christie, Len Downton, Lathem, Mr E. Butcher (committee member) and Charlie Kay (a keen athlete who attended several Olympic Games for his holidays).

Fred Damen was the Club Secretary during the late 1930's, until the outbreak of World War II. I managed to borrow the Minute

THE NINETEEN-THIRTIES

Book, which Mr. Damen kept for the Harriers some years ago.

I remember reading in that minute book that the Harriers winter road-racing programme included weekly races held from St Paul's Church Hall. The routes were similar to those described earlier for Weymouth YMCA Harriers back in 1911!

The cross-country course was on Lodmoor.

Races were often run as Handicaps.

A name that cropped up in those pre-war races was a young Ross Keel, who became one of the Harriers top runners after the war.

This Minute Book finished in 1939, when the Club temporary disbanded as all the active young men were otherwise engaged.

However, athletics continued in some form or other during those war years.

THE NINETEEN-THIRTIES

4. THE NINETEEN-FORTIES

In August 1942 the Vickers Armstrong Sports Ground (later AE Pistons and Wellworthy Engineering) at Ferrybridge was the venue for an athletics meeting.

Various track and field events were held, including a tug of war and a veterans' handicap 80 yd race. The oldest competitor was said to be 89 years old!

Also, with much military activity in the Weymouth area, many inter-service sports were held. I have no information on these events.

We do know that Ross Keel kept himself fit during the war, because we have it on record that he finished 3rd in an inter-service one mile race in 1943. Of interest, the winner of that race was none other than Sidney Wooderson, National one mile record holder and National cross-country champion.

After the war, Ross took up long distance running with great distinction, representing the Harriers in the inaugural Isle of Wight marathon.

Actually, Ross ran in several Isle of Wight marathons, often finishing under 3 hours, which is some achievement in itself, as the course is one of the toughest in the country.

Ross took part in the Brockenhurst to Bournemouth races 4 times, but was best known for his meritorious runs in the Swanage 12 miles road race. Ross finished 2nd on one occasion and 3rd three times.

He represented Dorset County many times at cross-country events, also winning a bronze medal in the Dorset County 1 mile

THE NINETEEN-FORTIES

championship.

Ross Keel and Martin Cartwright jointly held the record for the Chesil Beach Run, which was run from West Bay to Portland, for many years. I believe the official record for this run is held by Bob Pape. Pape was a Navy runner, active in the area in the 1960's.

As Ross became older, he achieved the ultimate in long-distance running by competing in a Land's End to John O'Groats 1000 miles race. Ross completed the distance in 17 days, which unfortunately put him just out of the prizes. However, he did well to start, let alone finish, because he had difficulty in finding a sponsor, and for much of the race he was badly injured. Ross sadly died aged just 63 years old in 1983.

His wife, Beryl, donated the "Ross Keel Memorial Centenary Cup" which is awarded annually to the year's outstanding Harrier. (That Cup and this History mark the Centenary of Weymouth St Paul's Harriers.).

5. THE POST WORLD WAR II PERIOD

In 1948 the Harriers were officially reformed after the Second World War, although in practice it had never officially been disbanded. But because of the dispersal of athletes, there was a need to sort out a committee and programme.

It was during the next decade that the Harriers started to rebuild a strong club. Ross Keel took on the job of Club Captain, and in the team was a youthful, Brian Dunn, his younger brother, Charles and Ben Grubb. Of interest, Brian Dunn won the inaugural 'Shave Cross' hill race in 1947!

Figure 11: St. Paul's Harriers in about 1950. Youths and Seniors Group.

Back from left: Fred Damen, Brian Dunn, unknown, Charles Dunn, John Babb, Geoffrey Scadden, John Case, Brian Ayles, John Savidge, Jack Gilbert, Frank Miller and Ernie Miller. Front from left: Fred Kay, Charlie Kay, Barry Burt.

THE POST WORLD WAR TWO PERIOD

Between 1950 and 1960 the Harriers were a strong force in the South-West.

The Harriers competed in inter-club cross-country and road races with Stadium AC (Portland Borstal Institute), the Junior Leaders Regiment at Bovington, Poole AC, Bournemouth AC, St Luke's College, Exeter, Osprey AC, various Royal Navy ships in dock at Portland, local army teams as well as the larger multi-club races such as Salisbury Round the Houses, Taunton '10' the Hampshire and Wessex cross-country leagues.

They also competed in the Dorset County Championships which were held in conjunction with Wiltshire.

Then, because of the small number of clubs in Dorset, many Harriers represented the county in the Inter-Counties' Championships.

Figure 12: c1955
Back Row: Brian Dunn, Richard Harris, Ross Keel
Front: Brian Ayles

Of interest, the Western Counties Cross-Country Championships

THE POST WORLD WAR TWO PERIOD

were held at Redlands in 1953.

The most notable and prolific runner of that period was Brian Dunn. If he was not competing for the Harriers in one of the above races, he was putting in medal winning runs for the Territorial Army cross-country team!

Ben Grubb joined the club whilst in the army at Bovington. Ben was an outstanding runner of that period, and went on to represent the UK on the track in the steeplechase.

Listed below are some examples of Harriers performances in the 1950s and 1960s.

1958: Harriers v BAC v RAPC I Griffiths, Gilbert, R Harris, R Keel, B Ayles, Wareham, Perryman, Mickell, Brown.

Johnstone-Browne 2½ m Handicap: 1 G Frampton, 2 B Dunn (scratch), 3 D Smith, 4 D Read. Timekeeper: Gilbert and AJ Browne, Handicapper: FJ Miller.

1959: Johnstone-Browne Handicap Cup 2½ miles B Dunn off scratch beat the record set by both K Tucker 1933 and J Shepstone 1935. Handicap placings were: B.J. Rutherford, R Caswell, G Brookfield, R Harris, M Andrews, P Talbot, B Ayles, C Dunn, R Keel, H Dowell, M Hallett, A J Browne.

Taunton '10': 1 B Grubb (51min 35sec), 4 B Dunn (53min 52sec).

Club Championships: 1 B Dunn, 2 C Dunn, 3 B Ayles, 4 R Harris, 5= H Dowell and R Keel. Juniors: R Caswell, B Rutherford, P Talbot.

The Harriers competed in track and field meetings against teams from Bournemouth, Poole and Yeovil in the 1950s.

For example some results from a match with Poole Harriers in 1959:

Men - B. Ayles 1st 440 yds., B. Dunn 1st 1 mile, G. Frampton 2nd 2 miles, R. Guest 1st shot (45 feet), 1st discus (114 feet 8 inches). Gavin Frampton represented Dorset in the six miles race in the Inter-Counties AAA Championships at the White City track in London. The race was won by Gordon Pirie with Gavin a lap behind.

Ladies - M. Clarke 2nd 100 yds., A. Spurrell 1st 220 yds., G. Dean 1st discus (76 feet 3 inches)

THE POST WORLD WAR TWO PERIOD

Figure 13: 1957 - Portland
Brian Dunn winning 1 mile race

Figure 14: 1956
Dorset County C.C., Hardye's School, Dorchester
Richard Harris, Charlie Dunn, Brian Ayles, Harry Dowell, John Watling

THE POST WORLD WAR TWO PERIOD

Richard Harris was a very keen member of St Paul's Harriers. He lived in Lyme Regis so always had travel to race with his team mates. He joined the Harriers in 1952 and ran a 4 min 32 sec mile, aged 16.

He had Dorset County golds as a youth and junior from distance of 440 yds to 1 mile.

In 1956, he was the 2nd senior 1 mile, and in 1957, 1st senior 1 mile.

In 1958, he was in the 1st Dorset Police Sports ½ mile. He also competed regularly in cross-country and road races as well as representing Dorset at athletics and rugby.

In 1959, the year he died, aged 22 years, he was placed 4th in the Dorset AAA's 1 x mile.

Figure 15: 1958 - Dorset County C.C. Wyke Camp

Harry Dowell, Brian Dunn, Richard Harris, Martin Cartwright, Ross Keel, Unknown, Brian Ayles, Ben Grubb, Charlie Dunn.

THE POST WORLD WAR TWO PERIOD

Figure 16: Weymouth St. Paul's Harriers

First in Dorset County AAA's Cross Country Championships.

Colin Fry kneeling third right and Brian Dunn kneeling third left and Derek Thomas kneeling second right.

In the Harriers colours that year was Colin Fry, who older runners will have recognised as Chief Inspector Fry who used to be on BBC's "Crime Watch".

Colin Fry represented the club for the years 1958 - 1963 and he not only won the Dorset Cross-Country title as a youth but also came fourth in the Southern Counties Cross-Country.

Figure 17: 1958 - Weymouth Carnival Road Race
Brian Dunn, Ben Grubb, Carnival Official and Ross Keel

THE POST WORLD WAR TWO PERIOD

Figure 18: 1959 - Taunton '10' Team Winners

Back: Brian Dunn, Ben Grubb.
Front: Ross Keel, Dave Smythe

The Richard Harris Cup is presented to the 1st individual in the Harriers' annual 10 mile road race (see below).

1960 Club Officers: President O.F. Linnett, Chaiman F.J. Miller, Sec. A.J. Brown, Treasurer M. Cartwright, Fixtures sec. B. Ayles, Captain C. Fry, Committee P. Gill, J. Gilbert, C. Kay, D. Cole, B. Dunn.

THE POST WORLD WAR TWO PERIOD

Figure 19: 1963/64 - SWCCC Tophies

Robert Skinner, Brian Dunn, Roy Honebon, Mary Scadden, Pete Clarke and Alan Browne

Figure 20: Taunton South West County Championships

Colin Fry, Len Horlock, Brian Dunn, Harry Dowell, Jeremy Sampson.

6. CUP AND TROPHIES

The Harriers have over the years owned a number of magnificent trophies. Some have already been mentioned and date back to the beginning of the century.

Unfortunately, many have gone missing. Nevertheless, it is worth recalling them, because they are part of the history of the Harriers.

The Hurdle Challenge Cup

This was presented to the 1st St Paul's Harrier home in the annual 10 mile road race. It is now renamed as the TG Copp Cup, having been represented to the Harriers by Brian Copp, following the death of his father who won it outright. This trophy is currently presented to the Harrier who is judged to have given the best performance over the year.

The Weatheral Cup

This was also mentioned earlier, seems to have disappeared, and I have no further information about it.

The Johnstone-Browne Cup

The Johnstone-Brown Cup, was presented to the Club in 1932, to replace the TG Copp Cup for the Club's road running champion, for races of 6 miles distance.

One name engraved is G.R Lathem., for the years: 1934 (30min.10sec); 1935 (29min.36sec); 1936, (30min.27sec); 1937 (30min.49sec); 1938 (29min.30sec).

The time of 29 min 30 sec is excellent, even by today's standards. Brian Dunn has won this cup at least seven times according to news cutting reports.

Also Ben Grubb won it on several occasions.

This is now presented to the Club's 10 mile road race champion.

The Loyalty Test Cup

This was presented to the Harrier who was considered by the Committee to have put most effort into club activities during the year. This cup was presented in 1929.

Winners included : W. Christie (1930), K. Tucker (1931), F. Damen (1932) , K. Tucker (1933) , G. Lathem (1934), R.J.G. Shepstone and A. Legg (1935), G. Lathem (1936), F. Hyde (1937), G. Lathem (1938), M. Babb (1952), B. Dunn (1958).

Rev Martin Fisher Cup

(No details are available)

The Hambro Cup

This was presented by Col. Angus Hambro, well known in the county as a Conservative MP from 1886, and as a Unionist MP, 1910-1918. This cup was presented for inter club running competition between South Dorset clubs.

The Richard Harris Cup

This is presented to the individual winner of the Weymouth 10 miles road race-championship.

Recent winners have been:

1962 JR Edwards, Bristol AC

1963 JR Edwards, Bristol AC

1964 DS Crooke, Torbay AC

1965 DS Crooke, Torbay AC

1966 JR Edwards, Bristol AC

1967 BJ Watson, Bournemouth AC

1968 IS MacIntosh, Ranelagh AC

1969 D Francis, Westbury Harriers

1970 D Francis, Westbury Harriers

1971 B Lewis, Southampton AC

CUPS AND TROPHIES

1972 D Collins, Plymouth AC

1973 B Plain, Westbury Harriers

1974 H Chadwick, Bournemouth AC

1975 D Francis, Westbury Harriers AC

1976 C Carthy, HMS Osprey, Portland

1977 B Heath, Royal Marines

1978 P Russell, WSPH

1979 P Russell, Bournemouth AC

1980 S Walker, Basildon AC

1981 J Boyes, Bournemouth AC

1982 J Boyes, Bournemouth AC

1983 J Boyes, Bournemouth AC

1984 P Critchlow, WSPH

1985 P Russell, Bournemouth AC

1985 P Russell, Bournemouth AC

1986 P Russell, Bournemouth AC

1987 R Hesledon, Royal Navy AC

1988 M Thomas, Poole Runners

1989 S Hendrie, Egdon Heath Harriers

1990 J Boyes, Bournemouth

1991 P Clark, Poole AC

The Babb Cup

This was presented to the club by John Babb in 1959 to the senior men's club track and field champion. Winners were: B. Ayles, 1957; 1958; M Cartwright, 1959.

No further names were engraved until recent years.

I believe that John Babb was a former headmaster of Weymouth Grammar School.

The Parry Gill Cup

CUP AND TROPHIES

The Parry-Gill Cup was presented to the club by Mrs. Parry-Gill in memory of her son who died about 1960. This cup is presented annually to the winning team in the Weymouth 10 miles road race championship.

Johnstone-Browne Handicap Cup.

Presented for handicap road races over a 2½ mile course. (Now missing).

Scarisbrooke Cup.

(No details are available)

Radford Shield

A young athletes' team trophy.

Ron Jones Cup

Boys Team trophy. Ron Jones was a former club President

D Bucke Cup

Colts cross-country. Dave Bucke was a former club President.

HG Whittaker Trophy

Ladies team trophy.

Dorset Regiment Cup:

(No details are available)

Darch Challenge Trophy

Awarded for annual competition for young walkers.

T.G Copp Cup

This is a separate cup to the one mentioned above, and was presented annually for the junior cross-country champion. The last record was in 1978 (M. Dyble).

Ladies Championship Shield

Presented in 1979, by M Nolan, a former club treasurer, for the best performance by a club member.

7. THE NINETEEN SEVENTIES

Some Notes About The 'Weymouth 10'

As mentioned earlier, a 10 mile race has been run annually at intervals throughout the Club's history. The first recorded time in 1904 was 62 min 23 sec. Over the years, the course for this race has changed many times.

The early races were over 'out-and-back' routes, which are not popular today.

The first of the present series of Weymouth "10s" in 1962 started and finished in the town centre.

Pete Clarke mentioned the Weymouth "10" in a small feature in the Road Runners' Magazine (1991). I have added these few extra notes which readers might find interesting:

In the first race, won by England cross-country international, John Edwards, there were other internationals taking part, including Frank Salvat (4th) and Ken Smith (Ireland). Also, there was Bob Pape, sometime President of the now defunct Road Runners Club and Martin Cartwright, who was Club Secretary for a while, and later President of the Southern Counties AAAs.

The first race was organised by another Club Secretary and former athlete Alan Brown. Alan was a County official in Scouting.

It is interesting to list the Club runners competing in that race:

Brian Dunn, 9th (56 min 02 sec); Ernie Newport, 20th (59 min 26 sec); J Sampson, 33rd; Len Horlock, 43rd (Len competed for the Club for over 20 years); Harry Dowell, 48th.

In 1963, Lt. Col CF Linnett the Club President, presented the Parry-Gill Cup for the second time to Bristol AC.

Brian Dunn was 3rd that year (53 min 46 sec).

The Club was not to win the team race until 1971: Geoff Hebburn (awarded an MBE in 1999), Brian Dunn, Pete Clarke and Dave Tizzard were the scorers.

Interestingly, that year, inaugural Young Athletes' races were held: Tim Caswell and Roy Honeybon (colts), Peter Russell, Andy Jennings and Richie Taylor (Youths).

The 1970s

Brian Dunn won the over-40 veteran prize in the Weymouth '10' in 1975 (54 min 30 sec). This time is good which matches or betters times set by the Harriers' current veterans! Tony Coleman has been runner-up in this race on three occasions. Brian Dunn competed in this race until 1995.

These were halcyon years for the Harriers, with excellent team performances and individual placings for road running, cross-country and track. Also, the race-walking section was formed by the late Harry Callow.

Harry Callow, had then recently moved to the area after setting up Trowbridge Harriers. Harry was a strong supporter of the Harriers through thick and thin. His interests in race-walking are legendary, both as a coach and as a race-walking referee, but he started out as an athlete on the track and cross-country with many successes.

Most people knew Harry as the long serving Club President but he knew a lot about all aspects of athletics, especially the politics of the sport. He served on County, Area and National Committees, and was very forthright to state a point, especially in defence of race-walking and St Paul's Harriers.

Harry Callow did so much for the Harriers behind the scenes and he should go down in the annals of athletics history as a great clubman, who had a fervent support of race-walking.

Harry died in 1989 when over 90 years old!

THE NINETEEN SEVENTIES

Figure 21: Harry Callow - long time President

Examples Of The Depth In The Season 1973/4

Hon. Sec. and Treasurer: Rod Porter

Brian Dunn, was still a force to be reckoned with in the 1970's, both over cross-country and on the road. However, there were a number of young runners starting to show their mark who were after his crown. For example, Pete Russell and Tony Coleman, two of the Club's most talented athletes, as you will read later on.

Then there were Mike Baggs and Pete Clarke, two runners who put the Club on the long distance road running map.

Most readers will only know Pete Clarke for his coaching, track and field performances and cross-country running exploits, and probably he will go down in the history of the Club as the person who introduced dozens of young people to athletics, through the schools' system.

However, up to 1991 Pete had run more marathon races than any other Club member with some credible times around the 2½ hr mark.

He also competed in several "ultra-distance" races, including the 54 mile London-Brighton race and the "Two Bridges" race in Scotland. Of course, as a track and field competitor, Pete Clarke has (and still does) compete in all events, if needed.

In fact, it is this motivation, and setting an example to younger athletes as well as his coaching and committee work that he has, and is, a centre-pin member of the Club.

Pete Clarke also played an important role in local and county schools' athletics, including helping organise National Schools' Cross-Country Championships in Weymouth, County Team Official, Starter and co-organiser of the annual Dorset schools' trip to Percy (France).

Some of the young athletes he either coached or encouraged have gone on to be County champions, and compete in the All England Schools Athletics or cross-country finals. One young athlete who reached those heights, with encouragement from Pete Clarke, was Billy Quinn.

Billy Quinn won nearly every local, County and Southwest cross-country championship that there was between 1974 and 1977. He also won many young athletes' road races, which were popular in the 1970's. Besides that, he was pretty good on the track at 1500 m and 800 m distances.

His outstanding ability was shown in the Salisbury young athlete's road race where he came home an easy winner from Johnathan Richards and Dave Buzza, both of these athletes went on to become Internationals and in the latter case, an Olympian.

Quinn was backed by a bunch of enthusiastic and talented runners. Notably, Neil Coleman, Neil Price, Martin Dyble, Steve Self, Mike Dethick, Les Drage, Garry Conning, Mike Nolan, Vaughan Price, and Bayard Lane.

A glimpse at just one of the race-meeting results for 1978 revealed the following:

THE NINETEEN SEVENTIES

At Trowbridge, Youths; N Coleman 3rd, L Drage 5th, M Dethick 6th, 1st team. Boys; B Quinn. 1st, N Price 2nd, S Self 12th, M Dyble 19th, 1st team. Colts; B Lane 7th, V Price 26, M Nolan 29th, J Lane 32nd, team 4th.

For the 10 mile race that day, Tony Coleman (53 min 12 sec) 13th, Pete Clarke (55 min 54 sec) 34th,

Mike Baggs (55 min 28 sec) 28th, Brian Dunn (55 min 40 sec) 31st (1st Vet) and Keith Bartlett (57 min 00 sec) 41st, team 3rd.

Figure 22: Trowbridge 10 mile race
Len Horlock and Dave Bucke

THE NINETEEN SEVENTIES

Figure 23: From left: John Bolton, Pete Russell and Tony Coleman after winning the Yeovil AC 10 mile road race.

So far, in this history, there has been little mention of the ladies of the club. An outstanding female athlete was Carole Smith.

Carole joined the club in the early 1970's. She was the local schools champion at hurdles but the Club soon found out that her athletic talents were extensive.

She could run, jump and throw and her all round abilities meant that she has been, and is probably, the most consistent and loyal female athlete in the history of the club.

When she was studying away from Weymouth, she had a short spell with our close rivals, Bournemouth AC.

Apart from that break, Carole has competed for the Club and served on its committee for many years.

THE NINETEEN SEVENTIES

Figure 24:

Carole Smith, all round athlete and long serving club member.

Not only is Carole an all round athlete, she is a competitive swimmer, cyclist bi-and tri-athlete and hockey player. She has competed for Dorset and the Civil Service at athletics and hockey.

Currently, her talents are again in demand as a Veteran International athlete.

Throughout the 1970s, the track and field team was making its mark at county, and even for some individuals, at national level.

There was excellent parental help from George Self, Mike Nolan, Ron Jones, Evelyn Morris and Irene Abery.

Irene followed Ailene Wood as Secretary for a while. At the end of the decade, notable athletes included Rachel Coton and Gina Morris, both excellent long-jumpers who represented County and Area and on numerous occasions.

Both later went on to gain Junior International vests.

Denise Abery (now Apsden) started as an enthusiastic athlete on the track and at cross-country running. Eventually, she took up race-walking under the guidance of Harry Callow, and became the Club's leading lady, race-walker.

Other regulars of that period were Diane Critchlow, Lisa Bucke, Justine Morris, Anne Cody, Sue Cody, Anne Linden, Diane and Jackie Treloar, Jane Aston.

Young male athletes around then included Steve Bucke, John White, Geoff Cotter, Mark Dent, Robert Russell, Simon Angus, Mark Goldstone and Shane Scadding.

Of the girls, sisters Debbie and Jackie Treloar became County

Champions at javelin and discus. Debbie won the County Sword of Merit for outstanding javelin throwing.

Lisa Bucke and Diane Critchlow competed for Dorset County, and All-England Schools at Cross-country. Diane went on to run cross-country and 1500 m at National Schools and club level. In fact, she broke numerous county and area records at 1500 and 800 m, and was one of the most out-standing track and cross- country athletes the Club has produced.

For the youths, Shane Scadding competed at 800 m in the All-England Schools' championships.

Figure 25: 1970s – Weymouth St. Paul's Harriers

Brian Osborne, Andy Matthews, Brian Dunn, Tony Coleman, Steve Bucke, unknown, unknown, Kevin Parr-Burman, unknown, John Kenwood, Keith Bartlett, Keith Honisett and Pete Avery (Vice-Chairman and benefactor of the club)

THE NINETEEN SEVENTIES

The senior group of Club runners included, Pete Clarke, Dave Bucke, Phil Gibbs, John Bolton, Keith Bartlett, Mike Baggs, Brian Dunn, Paul Critchlow, Eddie French, Pete Russell, Les Hallett, Mark Anthony, Dave White, Mike Amey, Brian Osborne, Steve Skinner, and Tony Coleman.

It is interesting to note that most of these athletes were road or cross-country runners.

Mike Baggs was a very strong long-distance runner, and he competed in the London to Brighton 54 miles race, finishing 3rd on one occasion in a time of 5 hr 59 min.

He was 4th in the Woodford-Southend 44 mile race in 4 hr 15 min 51 sec, an exceptional time.

Mike also ran a fast marathon (2 hr 26 min 11 sec.

He also achieved a time of 53 min 31 sec for the 10 mile distance and 16 min 9.6 sec for the 5000 m race.

Mike used to run 40 miles over footpaths and bridleways on a Sunday!

Unfortunately, he had a bad accident involving being knocked down by a car, which put paid to his running career, because of injuries.

He died in 2015.

Figure 26:
1975 - Weymouth '10' Road Race. Mike Baggs standing at the start, injured

43

THE NINETEEN SEVENTIES

Figure 27: Mike Baggs representing the club in a road relay race.

Figure 28: Brian Dunn in the race as above.

THE NINETEEN SEVENTIES

Paul Critchlow was an outstanding middle-distance runner on the track (5000 m) cross-country and on the road. He ran a marathon in 2 hr 25 min, finishing 2nd in the prestigious Glasgow Marathon.

Whilst Paul was active in the Club, he coached a squad of young athletes, including his daughter, Diane, and later his younger daughter, Sue.

Pete Russell, like Mike Baggs, was an ex-Weymouth Grammar School runner, who went on through the age-groups to become a star runner for the Club, and later on for Bournemouth AC, where he eventually gained an International vest for the marathon.

Figure 29: 1979

Dave Bucke racing at Bournemouth in the Wessex League

Unfortunately, this run held in India was his last major race.

Pete was talented at cross-country running, winning many Wessex League and County races (1st aggregate: 1979-1982). He also won several County and Area titles, for 1500 m and 5000 m.

Tony Coleman was another highly respected runner, preferring cross-country and road running to track. Whilst with the Club, he was overshadowed by Pete Russell on some occasions.

Nevertheless, Tony won several 10 mile races, put up some good marathon and half-marathon times. His charismatic manner made him very popular with the athletes, but he did not always get on well with officialdom, which was a pity.

Later on, Tony was a founder member of Winfrith AC which later became the Egdon Heath Harriers.

This local club had grown from strength to strength, and certainly over the years has deprived WSPH from local road running talent.

THE NINETEEN SEVENTIES

The race walkers of this period included Kevin Baker, Denys Jones, Ron Jones, Charles Dunn and Geoff Hunwicks. Denise Abery was one of our outstanding girl race walkers.

Veteran's track and field championships even gaining interest.

Dave Bucke, in his first year as an over-40 vet (1978), ran 2 min 03 sec for 800 m in the Southern vet's at Southampton. The following year he clocked 2 min 05.7 sec for 800 m and 4 min 16.9 sec for 1500 m (for 3rd place), again in the Southern champs.

In the 1979/80 season Dave was 1st Veteran in the Wessex League cross-country and club veteran champion.

Figure 30: 1979 - Dave Bucke on the track

The 1979/80 season cross-country men's team members included: Tony Coleman, Brian Dunn, John Bolton, Mike Anthony, Keith Bartlett, Pete Clarke, Mike Baggs, Les Hallett, Mike Amey, Dave White, Pete Russell, Dave Bucke, Mike Anthony, Mick Reed, R. Brown, Len Horlock, Phil Gibbs, Paul Critchlow, Eddie French, Andy Bevan, Andy Nolder, Steve Self, Andy Jennings, Mike Dethick, Les Drage, Garry Connings, Billy Quinn, Neil Price and Mark Dyble.

Juniors included Neil Coleman, Mark Goldstone, Rob Harris, Lee

Connolly, Simon Angus, B. Lane, Steve Bucke, Mark Dent, J. Lane and Mike Nolan.

Of course, they did not all turn out for every race.

Nevertheless, there was depth in numbers.

A final note for the 1970's, was a letter from Mr. Ray Curtis, informing the club that it could hold races on his fields off Markham road.

Figure 31: 1979 - Club athletes received championship awards
Presented by Mr. Charles Woolford
Back: Pete Clarke, Kevin Baker, Charles Dunn
Middle: Natasha Faulkner, Louise Bucke, Charles Woolford, unknown, Gina Morris
Front: all unknown

THE NINETEEN SEVENTIES

8. THE NINETEEN EIGHTIES

The 1980's were the turning point for athletics in the UK. Although most of the events that caught the public's attention were far removed from grass roots clubs like WSPH and AC, there were some "knock-on" effects.

Marathon running was one event that captivated even the most unfit person's attention. Local interests were initially geared to the Portland marathons, so ably organised by the Royal Manor of Portland AC.

The Harriers were well represented in these races, giving the opportunity for many to have their first attempt at the 26+ miles. Club winners of this race, included Mike Baggs and Paul Critchlow.

1980

Paul Critchlow ran the Glasgow Marathon in 2 hr 25 min 1984 which might still make him the club's fastest marathon runner.

On the track, in 1980, Chris Coleman finished 7th in the Southern AAA's octathalon, despite being 2 years younger than the next competitor. Helen Lawley finished 2nd in the Southern girl's 2500 m race-walk. The County cross-country results for junior girls included 1, Diane Critchlow; 7th, Lisa Bucke; 11th, Rachel Pitman.

The Chesil Beach Race from the back of Ferrybridge (the Butts) to Chiswell, was organised by the Harriers for many years, and in 1980, some of the finishers included: 1, Pete Russell; 2, Paul Critchlow; 3, Tony Coleman; 4, Dave Wills 5, John Bolton; 1st Boy, Shane Scadding; 1st Girl, Diane Critchlow.

THE NINETEEN EIGHTIES

Figure 32: Dave Bucke with daughter Louise at the finish of the Chesil Beach Race.

1981

In 1981, the above athletes continued to shine, but notable performances were set by Jason Hawkins, 1st Colt in the Chippenham to Calne race walks, with Darren Mileham 4th.

Diane Critchlow was 2nd in the junior, SW CC Champs. 2nd in the all England Schools Champs at 1500 m.

1982

President:	Harry Callow
Vice Presidents:	R Jones, C Woolford, P Avery
Chairman:	D Bucke
Vice Chairman:	G Hunwicks
Secretary:	I Abery
Treasurer:	G Hunwicks
Social Sec:	P Dunning
Cross-Country Sec:	D Bucke
Juniors and Ladies:	T Faulkner

THE NINETEEN EIGHTIES

Club Captain Men:	P Critchlow
Ladies' Captain:	C Smith
Cross-Country Capt:	J Bolton.
Race Walking Capt:	R Jones
Junior Rep:	P Hall
Committee:	W Mileham, J Critchlow, B Copp, P Clarke
	T Coleman
Cross-Country Team Manager:	
	Olive Baggs.

The Club men's cross-country champion was Dave Wills, with Paul Critchlow 2nd and Tony Coleman; 3rd. The 1st Veteran was Len Horlock; 1st junior man, Robert Russell, 2nd Steve Bucke, 1st Youth, S Richardson; 2nd, Jon Kenwood ; 3rd, Patrick Hall.

Tony Coleman had an outstanding year: 3rd Jurd x-country 5 mile, 5th Mayflower 10 mile, 6th Petersfield 10 mile, 8th Bath half-marathon, 3rd Bath 10 mile, 3rd Swanage 12 mile, 2nd Somerton 20 km and 1st Melksham half marathon!

Marathon rankings: 1. M. Baggs 2 h 41 mins 12 sec Isle of Wight Marathon. This was ranked 1st because the course is extremely hard and one of the toughest in the country.

Other names with times included: J Bolton 2 hr 33 min; P Critchlow 2 hr 36 min; T Coleman; 2 hr 39 min 59 sec; L Horlock 2 hr 43 min 10 min; S Skinner 2 hr 45 min 31 sec; D White 2 hr 48 min; P Clarke 2 hr 48 min 34 sec; P Etheridge 2 hr 56 min; J Kenwood 3 hr 01 min; K Hunnisett 3 hr 03 min; D Bucke 3 hr 04 min; A Crane (Lady) 3 hr 25 min.

THE NINETEEN EIGHTIES

Figure: 33
Collage of St. Paul's Harriers in 1982

On the track, Diane Critchlow set a new Club record for the Girls (Under-15) 1500 metres 4 min 36.8 sec. Debbie Treloar, an Intermediate (Under-17) record for discus, 38 min 50 min, shot, 9.12 metres. Molly Heinrich, Girls shot, 9.36 metres. Darren

THE NINETEEN EIGHTIES

Mileham, (Colt Under-13) 2000 metres walk, 12 min 23.5 sec.

Race walking. The Harriers were very strong in this section: Geoff Hunwicks (6 miles, 46 min 27 sec); Denys Jones (7 miles, 52 min 02 sec and 1 mile, 6 min 42 sec); K Baker (20 miles, 2 hr 55 min 33 sec); D. Abery (3 km, 17 min 43 sec).

Also featuring were: Charlie Dunn, W. Street, B. Copp, J. Powell, T. Mileham and D. Edwards.

1983

Of note in 1983, was the continuation of fine running by John Bolton. His 1st place in the Wessex Marathon, 2 h 33 min 12 sec, to Tony Coleman's 2nd place (2 hr 36 min 50 sec) then 5th place in the March Hare cross-country race at Porton Down, again beating Tony Coleman (6th) and many other good club runners, was a good start to the year.

Mostly, up to that point, Coleman had beaten Bolton.

In 1983, there were 13 Harriers inside 3 hours for full Marathon held at Portland:

J. Bolton, 2 hr 33 min 12 sec   T. Coleman, ; 2 hr 36 min 50 sec

B. Dyke, 2 hr 43 min 30 sec   P. Clarke, 22 hr 49 min 58 sec

D. White, 2 hr 51 min 41 sec   D. Symonds, 2 hr 52 min 12 sec

D. Bucke, 2 hr 54 min 28 sec   M. Goldstone, 2 hr 56 min 06 sec

K. Parr-Burman, 2 hr 59 min 05 sec

Other marathon results were:

P. Critchlow, 2 hr 35 min 00 sec   K. Bartlett, 3 hr 00 min 06 sec

J. Kenwood, 3 hr 04 min 34 sec,   J. Mogg, 3 hr 09 min 17 sec

K. Hunnisett, 3 hr 10 min 10 sec   S. Bucke, 3 hr 11 min 10 sec

R. Read, 3 hr 14 min 07 sec;   B. Fry, 3 hr 24 min 17 sec

M. Moore, 3 hr 35 min 52 sec;   N. White, 3 hr 36 min 21 sec;

R. Blackford, 3 hr 48 min 34 sec;   P. Avery, 3 hr 55 min 48 sec;

A. Mursell, 4 hr 24 min 22 sec   B. Copp, 5 hr 15 min 01 sec.

At least twenty-four club runners ran the distance that year!

The following four pictures show club members taking part in the Portland Marathon in the early 1980s.

THE NINETEEN EIGHTIES

Figure 34: John Bolton in the Portland Marathon

Figure 35: Portland Marathon. Andy Matthews in the white T-shirt.

THE NINETEEN EIGHTIES

Figure 36: Steve Bucke in the Portland Marathon

Figure 37: John Bolton in the London Marathon.

THE NINETEEN EIGHTIES

Figure 38: Left to right - Steve Bucke, John Bolton and Jim Brumfield relaxing after the London marathon.

Figure 39: A jubilant John Bolton at the finish of the Weymouth 10 mile road race.

Figure 40: Paul Critchlow leading in the National Veterans road relay race at Sutton Coldfield.

A colt's team from the Harriers was 1st in the Chippenham-Calne Walks (D. Mileham, McFarlane and Green).

In 1984, Diane Critchlow continued to shine on the track at 800 and 1500 metres. She finished 2nd in the Southern Counties 800 metres in 2 min 14.4 sec.

At this same event Debbie Treloar won the prestigious "Wilkinson Sword" award for best female performer in the Dorset Track and Field Championships (1st javelin, discus and shot).

Denys Jones came 1st; Kevin Baker 2nd and Geoff Hunwicks 3rd in the men's 3 km County Walk. Daren Foley was 1st in the Youth's 100 metres. Gina Morris was 1st senior ladies long jump and Sue Critchlow came 1st in the Junior Ladies 1500 metres with Amy Shepherd 1st in the Girls long jump and 1st in the 100 metres.

Helen Curtis was 1st in the ladies high jump. For the veterans: Dave Bucke, 2nd 800 metres.

In fact that year the Club won 11 golds, 12 silvers and 15 bronze

THE NINETEEN EIGHTIES

medals at the County Championships.

It is interesting to note that Bernard Fry (a busy dairy farmer at Little Bredy) was 3rd scorer for the Club in a Wessex League Cross-country race. When Bernard brought the cows in for milking he ran around the fields wearing Wellington boots.

He regarded that activity as his training runs!

1985

Officials:

President:	Harry Callow,
Chairman:	Stan Curtis,
Hon. Sec.	Diane Crumbleholme,
Treasurer:	Geoff Hunwicks,
Race Walking Sec.	Ron Jones,
Road Running:	Dave Bucke,
Track and Field:	Irene Abery,

There was a decline in numbers of road-runners in the Club compared with the five previous years. This was the result of the setting up of a rival club, Egdon Harriers, and the consequential defection of a number of our Harriers to that club.

For the ladies, Jo Dering put in a few good performances such as 2nd in Wessex Leagues (intermediate).

Sue Critchlow posted several 1sts in Wessex Leagues (Junior), backed by Anita Waddingham. Her father, Mike Waddingham was 1st o/45 vet. in the Wessex League.

Minor girls included Louise Bucke, Amy Shepherd and Alison Appleby.

THE NINETEEN EIGHTIES

Figure 41:

Group of Harriers after a training session in Puddletown Forest

Back: Dave White, Sandra Coleman, Tony Coleman, unknown

Front: Keith Bartlett, Louise Bucke, Paul Critchlow, John Bolton

On the track, the Club again had a successful season.

Toby Smith, finished 1st over 100 metres and 200 metres in several colt's races. Lee Purnell, Matthew Paul and Nathan Hunnisett were outstanding at field events and hurdles.

In the younger girls age groups, Amy Shepherd, Louise Bucke, Angela Dunn and Natasha Faulkner covered all events.

In fact, these athletes were fine backing for the Club's senior ladies in the Womens' Southern League races.

There, Carole Smith, Sheri Eyles, Gina Morris, Denise Abery and the Critchlow sisters were regular competitors.

Howard Smith showed what a fine triple jumper he was going to be with his youth's debut of 13.12 metres.

THE NINETEEN EIGHTIES

Figure 42: Louise Bucke - An outstanding, all-round athlete pictured in 1985.

1986

Outstanding in 1986 was Paul Critchlow's 4th place in the prestigious Bournemouth Bay Half marathon (71 min 09 sec). Overall 923 runners finished!

John Bolton, 1st veteran and second overall in the Portland 10m road race in a time of 55 minutes! Jim Brumfield in 15th position,

THE NINETEEN EIGHTIES

followed by Keith Jarvis 17th, Andy Watling 18th, Chris Sharratt 33rd, Dave Symonds 34th, Bill Parsons 36th, Pete Clarke 39th, Brian Dunn 42nd (65 min 16 sec!), Ian Davies 58th, Phil Childs 55th, Steve Bucke 60th, Dave Bucke 66th, Norman White 82nd and John Parsons, 121st.

Helen Curtis high jumped 1.70 metres to win the Southwest School's title and that year was her 4th appearance in the National School's Champs.

At the Club's AGM, former European 400 metres gold medallist, John Wrighton, presented Esso 5 star awards to Louise Bucke, Natasha Faulkner, Wayne Banks, Stuart Lloyd, Darren Sherwood and Mark Puckett.

County winners included, (SL) Gina Morris, 100 metres, long-jump; Helen Curtis, high jump; Anita Waddingham, 3000 metres walk; D Treloar, javelin. (Int.L) Sue Critchlow, 3000 metres. (JL) Louise Bucke, 200 metres, long jump.

At the AGM, John Bolton was presented with the Johnstone-Browne cup and Pat Dunning the Loyalty Test Cup. Cross-country champions were: Louise Bucke (JL), Sue Critchlow (Inter), Carole Smith, (SL) Toby Smith, (Colt) Stuart Bowden (Boys), Simon Dunning (Junior), Roy Read (Sen. men) and veterans, John Bolton.

Stan Curtis retired as Club Chairman.

Club Secretary, Diane Crumbleholme, reported that she had written to the Borough Council Chief Executive about the need for an "all weather" track, and the Club was told that £1 million pounds had been put aside by Carters Developers!!

THE NINETEEN EIGHTIES

Figure 43: 1986 - Harriers Veterans team after the National 8 x 3½ mile road relay championships at Sutton Coldfield.

Pete Clarke, Paul Critchlow, Chris Reynolds, Bill Parsons, Paul Hawdon, Dave Bucke, Brian Dunn, Dave Symonds.

The Harriers competed in the National Veterans (over-40) 8x3 miles relay championships at Sutton Coldfield. The team of Paul Critchlow (15 min 33 sec), Pete Clarke (17 min 26 sec), Brian Dunn (19 min 02 sec), Dave Bucke (17 min 58 sec), Dave Symonds (17 min 10 sec), Bill Parsons (18 min 29 sec), Paul Hawdon (19 min 00 sec) and Chris Reynolds (17 min 49 sec) finished 72nd from 120 teams.

1987

In 1987, John Bolton continued his outstanding veteran's performances, for example 1st Dorset vet. in the Poole 10 km (32 hr 54 min).

Keith Jarvis, Dave Stevens and Paul Gould completed the team. Bolton was runner-up in the aggregate Wessex League (Veterans.)

It would be wrong to think that Brian Dunn was taking time out! Brian was competing regularly in cross-country races, often

THE NINETEEN EIGHTIES

finishing in the prizes for over-50 vets.

Figure 44: Dave Symonds - A good road runner

For the 1987/88 season the Club's veterans finished 2nd in the Wessex League. Dave Symonds, Dave Bucke and Pete Clarke were scorers.

However, the Club's younger male athletes were becoming depleted, especially over the country.

Even the female side of the Club was thin on the ground.

Only Louise Bucke, better known for her track and field exploits, turned out regularly and Clare Peters was making her debut as a Minor girl, to become another fine Club athlete on the track.

THE NINETEEN EIGHTIES

Figure 45: Bill Parsons

A loyal club runner from Bridport

At an open veterans meeting at Exeter, J. Bolton came 2nd in the 1500 metres race and 2nd at 5000 metres. D. Bucke was 1st in the 800 metres and 2nd in the 400 metres.

Louise Bucke was first in many League, County, South-West county events at high jump, long jump, hurdles and 800 metres.

She also scored 3900 points putting her second in a heptathlon at Bournemouth. Natasha Faulkner also competed in the heptathlon.

Louise Bucke received the Ladies Shield for being the outstanding track and field athlete of the year, Nick Palmer the Men's shield for track and field and John Bolton once more won the Johnstone-Browne Cup for best road runner.

In a rare and unusual occasion, the Ladies' section of the Harriers combined with Dorchester AC, and between them, won the prestigious Paulding Trophy at Bournemouth.

Stars for the club were Carole Smith (3 x 1sts), Louise Bucke (3 x 1sts), D Treloar, Anita Waddingham and Helen Curtis (1 first each).

The St. Paul's Harriers won promotion to Division 1 of the Westward League, following their magnificent win in the 2nd Division.

Six members of the Club were selected to represent Southwest counties - Kevin Baker, Denys Jones and Denise Abery (walks), Gina Morris and Sheri Eyles (long jump) and Louise Bucke (high jump).

A beach barbecue was organised by Jan Foley and Evelyn Morris.

Later that year, a disco-buffet evening was organised at the Wyvern Centre, Westham.

In the Southern veterans' Cross-Country championships held at Bournemouth, Bolton finished 6th (over-40), but 1st South-West Counties. Dave Symonds, finished 1st over-45 and Dave Bucke 3rd in the over-45 category..

Figure 46: John Bolton

One of the most consistent road and cross-country runners in the history of the club

1988

Paul Critchlow was experiencing the first of his leg injury problems. When he did compete, he was still a force to be reckoned with - a 1st veteran in a Wessex League at Chippenham, backed by Dave Bucke, Pete Clarke and Ray Blackford.

Dave Wrighton made one of his rare appearances in the "Round-the Lakes" races at Poole on Boxing Day, finishing 43rd, followed

THE NINETEEN EIGHTIES

by Dave Bucke 50th and 2nd over-50. Pete Clarke was 65th and Brian Dunn 75th.

Jo Dering was 1st junior lady in 55th place. (142 finishers).

The Portland 10 mile, showed that Bolton was 2nd veteran. (10th overall), closely followed by Dave Symonds 13th, Jim Brumfield 15th, Paul Gould 26th, Pete Clarke 38th, D Bucke 42nd, Chris Sharratt 44th, Patrick Hall 49th, Bill Parsons 60th, Steve Bucke 85th, Pete Mowlam 110th Christine Sharratt 112nd, W Parsons 118th and Pete Hammond 142nd.

On the Weymouth Marsh track, the Harriers were beaten by a strong Dorchester AC team in an Avalon League fixture. Outstanding for the Club was the 4 x 400 metres team of Dave Wrighton, Stuart Lloyd, Wayne Banks and Nick Palmer, which set a new Club record of 3 min 38.7 sec. Ken Houlberg and David Wrighton were 1st and 2nd in the 800 metres and 400 metres.

Once again Louise Bucke showed outstanding ability. Her 4th place in the "All England Schools" high jump (1.69 metres) was no doubt her best achievement. She also scored 3816 points for 11th in the "All England Schools" heptathlon.

At the County Championships, she took four intermediate age group titles (400 metres in 60.2 sec, 80 metres hurdles in 13.1 sec and high and long jumps).

Denise Abery and Denys Jones again retained their respective Walks titles.

Charles Dunn won the veterans walk title.

Other consistent competitors on the track were Paul Kingston and Nick Palmer - all field events and hurdles! Paul Kingston, from Litton Cheney, was a former All England Schools javelin champion.

He was also in the Irish Team Squad for the Winter Olympics, competing in the luge. Nick Palmer was a versatile athlete who could jump, sprint and hurdle well. When both Paul and Nick were available, they invariably competed in 11 or 12 events at a league match! Doug Veitch and Mark Puckett were strong supporting members of the team. It was in 1989 that a young Martin Peters was making his debut at javelin and pole vault. Martin later went on to be goalkeeper for Weymouth and later Bridport football teams.

THE NINETEEN EIGHTIES

Brian Dunn was honoured for 40 years Club loyalty as an active athlete, at a special presentation at the Club's annual dinner at the "Sea-Cow". The presentation was by Chairman, Brian Copp, who said "Brian had become a legend in his own lifetime" and wished him well for the future.

1989

This was the "official" centenary year of Weymouth St. Paul's Harriers.

President	Harry Callow,
Chairman	Brian Copp,
Vice Chairman	Dave Bucke,
Hon. Sec.	Margaret Mitchell,
Track and Field	Irene Abery,
Road Running	John Bolton,
Race Walking	Ron Jones,
Club Capt.	Tony Faulkner,
Ladies Capt.	Louise Bucke,
Treasurer	Evelyn Morris,
Junior Rep.	Stuart Lloyd,
Social Sec.	Jim Brumfield,
Southern League and Cross-Country	Dave Bucke
Schools' Rep.	Pete Clarke.
Vice Presidents	Mrs E. F. Damen, Messrs. R. Jones, C. Woolford, P. Avery,
Life Members	B. Dunn, S. Peters

THE NINETEEN EIGHTIES

Figure 47: Jim Brumfield (front right)

A former soccer player who took up running after his playing career ceased. A first class runner and clubman

There were no official celebrations to record the centenary and this is why this history has been compiled.

The Monday evening indoor fitness classes were held at Weymouth College Gymnasium. These classes were well attended. Jim Brumfield was elected social secretary, and organised a well attended dinner at the Sea Cow restaurant. The club applied for planning permission to build their own HQ on the Marsh.

The existing wooden club hut had to be demolished as it was frequently vandalised.

Weymouth and Portland Council advised the Club that it was unsafe. This old club hut was donated to the Harriers by Council. In fact it was really two wooden huts knocked into one!

A "100" savings club was started by Evelyn Morris, the club Treasurer. Club members could buy shares at a nominal price and every month there would be a draw for three prizes.

THE NINETEEN EIGHTIES

Charles Woolford, for a number of years the Club timekeeper, sadly passed away.

Charles was a qualified AAA's timekeeper, and had officiated at international meetings, as well as all local events including road and cross-country races.

John Bolton continued to make the headlines by being 13th overall in the Lanz quarter marathon, backed by Pete Clarke 52nd, Dave Bucke 82nd, Phil Childs 99th, Ray Blackford 112nd, Steve Bucke 120th, Dave Stevens 136, Brian Dunn 139th and Pete Hammond 358th. A total of 440 finished.

Figure 48: Tony Faulkner - Now better know as a club coach and veteran all-rounder, he was a regular member of the cross-country and road running team.

Portland 10m, results showed Bolton 9th (56 min 47 sec) backed

THE NINETEEN EIGHTIES

by Andy Watling 11th, Keith Jarvis 21st, Hedley Stone 29th, Dave Symonds 42nd, Pete Clarke 52nd, Dave Bucke 57th (1st over 50), Brian Vockins 81st, Brian Dunn 94th, Paul Hawdon 95th, Norman White 131st, Kevin Baker 160th (he walked!), and Pete Hammond 190th.

A total of 197 finished.

In the London Marathon, Pete Clarke ran an outstanding 2h 44m; John Bolton, 2 hr 55 min; Jim Brumfield, 2 hr 57 min; Phil Childs, 3 hr 09 min; Steve Bucke, 3 hr 50 min and Pete Hammond, 4 hr 29 min. Andy Stratton ran 2 hr 55 min in the Paris Marathon.

Overall positions in the Wessex League only included John Bolton, 3rd vet.

Did this demonstrate the lack of interest in cross-country running in the club at the end of its centenary?

Not quite!

The veterans finished first in this league!

Mark Puckett, mentioned early on in this history, was then running regularly for the Club.

In an Avalon League meeting over Curtis' fields, Clare Boichet finished 16th in the minor girls event. Carole Smith, finished 10th senior lady.

Ian Hughes was first Harrier home (65th) in the men's race, followed by Dave Bucke (85th), Ray Blackford (100th), Paul Hawdon (110th) and Pete Clarke (122nd).

The Harriers scooped several medals in the aggregate positions of the Wessex cross-country league. Veteran's team gained gold (John Bolton, Jim Brumfield, Dave Symonds, Pete Clarke, Dave Bucke and Tony Faulkner).

Also, as individuals, John Bolton 1st over-40; Dave Symonds 2nd over-45; Dave Bucke 3rd over-50.

Paul Critchlow was 6th fastest overall!

In the Combe Gibbet to Overton multi-terrain race John Bolton was 7th in 1 hr 37 min 41 sec, Dave Bucke 36th in 1 hr 53 min 12 sec; Phil Childs 37th in 1 hr 53 min 49 sec; Pete Clarke 39th in 1 hr 54 min 15 sec; Steve Bucke 85th in 2 hr 10 min 38 sec and Pete Hammond 128th in 2 hr 50 min 59 sec.

THE NINETEEN EIGHTIES

The walkers won the Trowbridge Traders Open 10 mile team race, (team Ron Jones, Kevin Baker, Denys Jones and Charles Dunn). Kevin Baker won the Nicola trophy, by leading from start to finish at Briantspuddle.

Charles Dunn and Ron Jones continued to put in fine performances.

On the track, Toby Smith was voted Man of the Match at a Men's Southern League meeting for an outstanding run in the 400 metres. Paul Kingston contested 10 events, winning the 110 metres hurdles, long jump, 3rd in the high jump, shot and discus.

Dave Bucke ran the 800 metres and sprinted to the other side if the track to run in the 3000 metres steeplechase. Martin Peters won the javelin.

At another League fixture, Ken Houlberg and Dave Wrighton teamed with Wayne Banks and Nick Palmer to once again break the Club record for the 4 x 400 metres (3 min 33.9 sec).

Jim Brumfield won the "B" 5000 metres. Dave Bucke finished 4th in the National Vets over-50 800 metres (2 min 15 sec), and Maurice Wood, 6th in the 400 metres.

Natasha Faulkner was improving her track and field performances in a number of events, and turning out to be a reliable asset to the team.

Louise Bucke continued to put up good performances on the track, especially at heptathlon, 400 metres, long and high jump, with national rankings in those events. At the AGM, she was the inaugural winner of the T.G. Copp Cup, (formerly, the Hurdle Cup for road-running!).

THE NINETEEN EIGHTIES

Figure 49: Ray Blackford - Ray took part in many track and field events to earn points for the club. He was a team member at cross-country events and ran eight Poole Marathon. He died in 2005

Mrs Damen, following the recent death of former Club athlete and secretary, Fred Damen, presented a shield in her husband's name to John Bolton, as the Club's outstanding cross-country and road runner for this year.

THE NINETEEN EIGHTIES

Evelyn Morris was presented with the Loyalty Test Cup for the 2nd year running. Margaret Mitchell was congratulated on her efficiency as Club secretary.

After 100 years, Weymouth / Westham St. Paul's Harriers and AC has not only proved to be a valuable asset to the Town, but has played its part in local, County, Area, National and International competition. Many of its officials have held administrative positions at most levels of athletics. It is due to the unselfish attitude of these officials and committee members that the Club has managed to survive to its Century.

Figure 50: Paul Hawdon - Veteran road runner

THE NINETEEN EIGHTIES

Figure 51: Clare Peters - She was talented at track and field events as well as cross-country running

Figure 52: Dave Bucke - Club runner and member of the club Committee for many years. President in 1992

The walkers won the Trowbridge Traders Open 10 mile team race, (team Ron Jones, Kevin Baker, Denys Jones and Charles Dunn). Kevin Baker won the Nicola trophy, by leading from start to finish at Briantspuddle. Charles Dunn and Ron Jones continued to put in fine performances.

On the track, Toby Smith was voted Man of the Match at a Men's

THE NINETEEN EIGHTIES

Southern League meeting for an outstanding run in the 400m. Paul Kingston contested 10 events, winning the 110m hurdles, long jump, 3rd in the high jump, shot and discus.

Figure 53: 1991: - Paul Kingston competed in the European winter games in the Luge event [2]

---

2. http://www.the-sports.org/paul-kingston-luge-spf209937.html

9. THE NINETEEN NINETIES

1990

The 1990/91 Officials were:

President	Harry Callow
Chairman	Brian Copp
Vice Chairman	Dave Bucke
Hon. Sec.	Val Palmer
Treasurer	Evelyn Morris
Track and Field	Irene Abery
Cross-Country	Dave Bucke
Captain	John Bolton
Race Walking	Ron Jones,
Schools' Liaison	Pete Clarke.

Many of the established athletes continued to compete in the 1990' including Nick Palmer, Paul Kingston, Howard Smith, Mark Puckett and Martin Peters. The old guard seemed to run on relentless, including Brian Dunn, John Bolton, Dave Symonds and dare I say it, Carole Smith!

There were many other names mentioned in press cuttings and some will be mentioned in the following examples of results for the early 1990s.

Figure 54: The 1990 Portland Five Mile Race.

Ladies' winner Carole Smith and Mike Feigham who won the race overall. Carole's time was 30 min 07 secs and Mike's winning time was 25 mins 55 secs.

New members included Mike Feighan, Abigail Bailey, Tom and Ruth Bochoit. Also their mother, Judith became a club member.

The biggest athletics event ever held in Weymouth took place. It was a stage of the Wessex cross-country league races on Markham and Little Francis Fields. The event was staged by the club. Over 800 athletes took part, from minor girls to veteran men and ladies. The course was exceptionally muddy.

Success came for Abi Bailey (2nd) in the under-13 age group. She was backed by Vicky Churchill (15th) and Clare Bosomworth (41st).

Clare Peters finished 4th in the under-17 girls group. Carole Smith, also 4th in the senior ladies. Mike Feighan,(10th), John Bolton (16th), Keith Jarvis (39th), Dave Symonds (51st), John McKie (76th), Mark Puckett (79th), Ray Blackford (94th), Dave Bucke (114th) and Norman White (118th).

Some road running results for the year.

Pete Clarke ran in a 100 km race in the town of Milton Keynes. His time was 10 hr 30 min.

John Bolton finished 10th from a thousand runners in the Bristol Half Marathon. His time was just over 75 min. This put him at 2nd over-40 veteran; a remarkable performance.

Figure 55: Mike Feigham running through Easton on the Portland Five Mile Race, 1990.

Further results on the road included: Mike Feighan, 6th in the Bournemouth 10 mile race in 50 min 58 sec; John Bolton, 13th in 52 min 31 sec.; Jim Brumfield, 31st in 56 min 14 sec.; Keith Jarvis, 56 min 41 sec; Hedley Stone, 57 min 09 sec.; John McKie, 58 min 12 sec and Pete Clarke 60 min 49 sec.

Pete Clarke also ran in the Snowdon Marathon recording a time of 3 hr 20 min.

Figure 56: 1990 - Start of the Weymouth 10 mile road race. 2nd Left: Tony Coleman (now running for Egdon Heath Runners) 4th Left: Mike Feighan who finished 2nd Long time sponsors of this event were Lanehouse Motors and John Starkey and Partners

On The Track

The Harriers were having a cracking time on the track in 1990. Especially, in the Southern Mens' League.

For example at St. Albans: Martin Peters broke the club record for the javelin (44.90 metres); Howard Smith won a triple jump in 13.76 metres. Paul Kingston competed in eight events, with 4 firsts, and 4 second places. Toby Smith won the 100 metres, 200 metres and 400 metres. Ray Blackford competed in the 400 metres hurdles, 800 metres, 1500 metres, 5000 metres and the 3000 metres steeplechase! Wayne Banks had a first in the 400 metres and Skipper, Tony Faulkner competed in five events.

To cap it all the Harriers won both the 4 x 100 metres and 4 x 400 metres relays.

A similar story unfolded in League matches at Swindon and Trowbridge. Doug Veitch broke the club record for the discus (34.48 metres).

There were plenty of active runners to call upon apart from those mentioned above for these senior men's events, e.g. Dave Wrighton, Andy Watlin, Dave Bucke, Pete Clarke and Nick Palmer.

Race Walking

The Nicola and Friendship races held at Briantspuddle under the strict organization by Harry Callow and Ron Jones were an important feature on the race walking calendar.

Weymouth walkers included Kevin Baker, Bill Lawrence, Ron Jones, Harry Harris and Charlie Dunn. Ron Jones also won races on the track for 3000 metres and 5000 metres in the S.W. Veterans meeting.

1991

The Harriers had another year of successes in most of the age groups.

Mike Feighan won the New Year's day road race at Broadstone (32 min 56 sec), John Bolton, 11th (35 min 54 sec), Jim Brumfield, 18th (37 metres 08 sec) and Pete Clarke, 49th to give the team 3rd place. However, later in the year, Mike Feighan ran his last race for the Harriers, having taken up an appointment in Devon. He finished in style, winning the Shaftsbury 6 mile race.

This was also Jim Brumfield's last year with the Harriers. He decided, after giving it some thought, to join up with Egdon Harriers.

This was a shame as Jim had been a very loyal athlete. He did continue for a while as a first claim member on the track. Nevertheless, there were more good results in the year.

Carole Smith finished first in the Tarrant Valley 6 miles road race. Gill Bucke, ran her first race for many years, finished 2nd in her age group in the same race.

Charlie Dunn won an 8 mile invitation race walk at Briantspuddle.

John Bolton was first over 45 year age in the National rankings for his 52m 31s in the previous year's Bournemouth 10 mile. He was also 1st veteran in a half marathon in Malta.

This was a fine year for Abi Bailey. She finished 1st in the Dorset and the South West Cross-Country Championships and was ranked 6th for her age group 1500m (4m 42s).

Clare Peters was County champion cross-country Intermediate girl. James Hampson, runner-up in the County Boys' race.

Good performances were made by Sarah Stanwix, Claire and Ruth Bochoit, Cathy Bosomworth, Vicky Churchill and Fay Hickman.

Over the years, there has been lots of speculation about a new all-weather running track and new head-quarters for St. Paul's

Harriers.

So far all has been fruitless.

However, this year (1991) planning permission was given for a new head-quarters building with changing rooms and showers. A special meeting was called on 15th February at Weymouth College to investigate ways to raise funds and the formulation of a self-build policy.

What happened to it?

Figure 57: 1991 – Brian Copp (Chairman) presents the T.G. Copp cup to Clare Peters for Best Performance

Figure 58: Club Secretary, Evelyn Morris received the Loyalty Test cup for services to the club.

Figure 59: *1991 - Weymouth 10 mile road race - 3rd front left: Paul Critchlow*

Figure 60: 1991 – Club Trophy Presentation

Weymouth and Portland Mayor, Alan Rendall, presented trophies to club members.

Back L to R: Paul Kingston, Claire Bochoit, Abi Bailey, Clare Peters, Natasha Faulkner, John Bolton.

Front L to R: Howard Smith, unknown, Ruth Bochoit, Vicky Churchill, Gina Morris, Tom Bochoit, Mayoress and Mayor

Figure 61: Southern Counties Championships
Left: Clare Peters 400 metres
Right: Natasha Faulkner, 2nd Triple Jump

Figure 62: Abi Bailey, an outstanding middle distance runner wins, beating the boys in the Weymouth Carnival Race 1991.

THE AUTHOR

David Bucke first took up 'serious' athletics around the age of fourteen.

He got involved in most track and field events whilst at Woking Athlete Club before moving on to the Guildford and Godalming Athletic Club.

On moving north he joined the Cambridge and Coleridge Athletic Club. He was the County Cross-Country Champion in 1965 and represented Cambridge in track and field events.

He joined the Weymouth St. Paul's Harriers in 1977 soon after moving to Weymouth in Dorset.

He held most of the committee positions over the decades and is a Life Member.

He is still actively running as he approaches his eightieth birthday.

INDEX

Avalon League Fixture, 66

Brasher, Chris, 12

Bristol Half-Marathon 1990, 79

Chesil Beach Race, 49

Chippenham-Calne Walks, 57

Cups and Trophies
    Babb Cup, 33
    Hambro Cup, 6, 14, 17, 32
    Hurdle Cup, 6, 17, 31
    Johnstone-Browne Cup, 25, 31, 61, 64
    Loyalty Test Cup, 14, 32
    Martin Fisher Cup, 32
    Parry Gill Cup, 34, 36
    Paulding Trophy, 65
    Richard Harris Cup, 29
    Ross Keel Memorial

    Centenary Cup, 22
    T.G. Copp Cup, 71
    Weatheral Cup, 17, 31

Curtis, Ray, 47

Dorchester Athletic Club, 18

Dorchester YMCA Harriers, 5, 6, 17

Dorset Constabulary Sports, 12

Dorset Police Sports, 5, 27

Dorset Track and Field Championships, 57

Feigham, Mike, 79, 80, 81

Glasgow Marathon, 45

Hambro, Col. Angus, 32

Hardye's School, Dorchester, 26

Hawdon, Mike, 62

Isle of Wight Marathon, 51

Lodmoor, 18
London Marthon 1989, 70
Marsh Road, Weymouth, 12
Members
  Abery, Denise, 46, 65, 66
  Abery, Irene, 41, 50, 58, 67, 77
  Anderson, W, 8
  Andrews, M, 25
  Angus, S., 41
  Appleby, A., 58
  Apsden, A. (nee Abery), 41
  Aston, J., 41
  Avery, P., 50
  Ayles, B., 24, 25, 26, 29, 33
  Babb, Fred, 15
  Bagell, R, 8
  Bagell, T, 8
  Baggs, M., 37, 39, 43, 49
  Bailey, Abi, 78, 85
  Baker, Kevin, 46, 47, 65, 70
  Banks, Wayne., 71
  Barret, W, 8
  Bartlett, C, 8
  Bartlett, K., 39
  Blackford, R., 53, 65
  Bochoit, Ruth., 78
  Bochoit, Tom., 78
  Boichet, Clare., 70
  Bolton, John, 59, 62, 64, 67, 77, 79
  Bosomworth, Cathy, 81
  Bosomworth, Clare, 78
  Brantingham, W, 8
  Bridgeman, S, 8
  Brookes, 18
  Brookfield, G., 25
  Brown, A.J., 29, 35
  Brown, R, 8
  Browne, A, 30
  Brumfield, Jim, 67, 68, 70
  Bucke, Dave, 40, 46, 50, 51, 57, 58, 61, 63, 64, 65, 67, 70, 71, 75, 77
  Bucke, Gill, 81
  Bucke, Lisa, 41
  Bucke, Louise, 47, 58, 59, 60, 61, 63, 64, 65, 66, 67, 71
  Bucke, Steve, 41, 53, 61, 70
  Bugler, George T, 7, 8
  Butcher, 18
  Callow, Harry, 36, 41, 50, 58, 67, 77, 80
  Cartwright, M., 22, 29, 33
  Caswell, R., 25
  Childs, Phil, 70
  Christie, 13, 18
  Churchill, Vicky, 78
  Clarke, Pete, 30, 36, 37, 38,

47, 67, 70
Cody, A., 41
Cody, S., 41
Cole, D., 29
Coleman, A., 37
Coleman, Tony, 45, 49, 51, 53
Condliffe, G., 3
Copp, Brian, 67, 77
Copp, T.G., 13, 14, 17, 18
Costello, T., 5
Coton, Rachel., 41
Cotter, S., 41
Crane, A., 51
Critchlow, Diane, 41, 45, 49, 50, 52, 57
Critchlow, Paul, 33, 45, 49, 51, 53, 57, 59, 60, 65, 70, 83
Critchlow, Sue, 45, 57, 61
Crumbleholme, Diane, 58, 61
Curtis, H., 57
Curtis, S., 58
Curtis, Stan, 61
Damen, F, 14
Damen, Mrs E.F., 67
Damers, F., 18
Damon, L.C., 3
Darch, 14, 18
Dent, M., 41

Dering, Jo, 58, 66
Dowell, H., 25, 26, 27, 30, 35
Downton, L., 18
Drage, L., 46
Dunford, 18
Dunn, A., 59
Dunn, Brian, 2, 23, 25, 26, 27, 28, 29, 30, 35, 37, 39, 69, 70
Dunn, Brian honoured for 40 years membership., 67
Dunn, C., 23, 25, 26, 46, 47
Dunn, Charles, 66
Dunning, Simon, 61
Dyble, M., 46
Etheridge, P., 51
Eyles, S., 59, 65
Faulkner, Natasha, 47, 64, 71, 84
Faulkner, T., 69
Feighan, Mike, 78, 79
Fellowes, Bill, 14
Fisher, Rev. M., 6, 7, 8, 13, 18
Fry, B., 53, 58
Fry, C., 28, 29, 30
George, W. G, 1
Gilbert, J., 29
Gill, P., 29

Gould, Paul, 62
Grubb, B., 23, 25, 28, 29, 32
Hall, M, 8
Hall, P., 51
Hammond, Pete, 2, 7, 66, 69, 70
Handal, 18
Harris, R., 24, 25, 27
Hawdon, Paul, 70, 73
Hawkins, J., 50
Hebburn, Geoff, 36
Heinrich, Molly, 52
Hibbs, 18
Hickman, Fay, 81
Hodge, Percy, 2, 11
Honebon, R., 30
Horlock, L., 30, 39, 51
Houlberg, Ken, 66, 71
Hughes, Ian., 70
Hunwicks, G., 46, 53, 57, 58
Hurdle, H.A., 5
Hutchins, Tom, 7
Jarvis, Keith, 62
Jones, Denys, 46, 66
Jones, J., 65
Jones, Ron, 41, 46, 50, 58, 67, 71, 80
Kay, C., 18, 29

Keech, T, 8
Keel, Ross, 21, 23, 24, 29
Kenwood, J., 51
Kingston, Paul, 66
Kunnisett, K., 51
Lathem, G.R., 18, 31
Lawley, H., 49
Linden, A., 41
Linnett, Lt. Col. C.F., 16, 29, 36
Lloyd, Stuart, 66, 67
Lovell, H. E, 8
Lovell, R, 8
McFarlane, 57
McKie, John, 79
Mileham, Darren., 50
Miller, F.J., 5, 13, 14, 18, 29
Morris, Evelyn, 41, 67, 77
Morris, Gina, 41, 47, 65
Morris, J., 41
Mursell, A., 53
Newport, E., 35
Palmer, F, 8
Palmer, Nick, 64, 66, 71, 77, 80
Palmer, Val, 2, 77
Parr-Burman, K., 53
Parry-Gill, 18
Payne, F, 8
Peters, Clare, 63, 74, 81,

82, 84
Peters, Martin, 66, 71
Porter, R., 37
Powell, John, 5
Prinhead, T, 8
Puckett, Mark, 8, 61, 66, 70, 77, 79
Quinn, Billy., 38, 39, 46
Read, R., 53
Reed, M, 8
Reynolds, Chris, 62
Russell, D., 36
Russell, P., 45, 49
Russell, R., 18, 41
Rutherford, B.J., 25
Sampson, J., 30
Scadden, M., 30
Scadding, Shane, 41, 42
Self, G., 41
Sharratt, Chris, 61
Sharratt, Christine, 66
Shaw, H, 8
Shepherd, A., 58
Shepstone, J., 25
Skinner, R., 30
Skinner, S., 51
Smith, Carole, 40, 41, 51, 59, 61, 65, 70, 77, 79, 81
Smith, H., 59
Smith, T., 71

Smythe, D., 29, 30
Spring, K., 18
Stanwix, S., 81
Stevens, Dave, 62
Stratton, Andy, 70
Symonds, D., 63
Symonds, J., 13
Symonds, W, 8
Talbot, P., 25
Tizzard, Dave, 36
Treloar, D., 41, 57
Treloar, Jackie, 41
Tucker, K., 18, 25
Uncles, L, 8
Vockins, B., 70
Waddingham, M., 58
Waddington, A., 58
Watlin, Andy, 80
Watling, John, 26
Welland, T, 8
Wellman, R.T., 8
Wheldon,H.H., 13
White, John., 41
White, Norman, 53, 61, 70, 79
Wills, Dave, 49
Wood, Maurice., 71
Woodwood, B, 8
Woolford, C., 47, 50, 67, 69

Wrighton, Dave, 65, 66, 80

Young, H, 8

Olympic Games, 1
   Percy Hodge wins 1920 3 km Steeplechase, 12

Paris Marathon 1989, 70

Pirie
   Gordon, 25

Poole Wheelers, 18

Porton Down, March Hare Race (1983), 53

Sharrat, Chris, 66

Snowden Marathon 1990, 79

South Dorset Labour Sports, 5

St. Paul's Church Boys Club, 7

Townsend, Joe, 2

Vickers Armstrong Sports Ground, 21

Warwick, H. D (Printer), 11

Wessex Marathon
   Won by John Bolton in 1983, 53

Western Counties Cross-Country Championships, 24

Westham St Paul's Harriers, 14

Westham St. Paul's Harriers, 5
   Formation, 5

Weymouth '10' Races, 35

Weymouth Bicycle Club, 3

Weymouth Carnival Road Race 1958, 28

Weymouth College, An History, 3

Weymouth Harriers
   Formation in 1889, 2

Weymouth Police Sports, 12

Weymouth Red Book, 2

Weymouth St. Paul's Harriers, 1

Weymouth Town Harriers, 5

Weymouth YMCA Harriers, 5, 9, 11

Wooden Hut, Demise of, 68

Wooderson, Sidney, 21

YMCA Harriers, 10

Printed in Great Britain
by Amazon